Lire à petits pas Niveau

Méthode Montessori pour apprendre à lire : du mot au livre

French English German Spanish - Welsh

family

famille

famille

familia

teulu

How big is your family?

---

man

homme

homme

hombre

dyn

This man is my dad.

---

hoe

houe

houe

azada

hoe

Use a hoe in the garden.

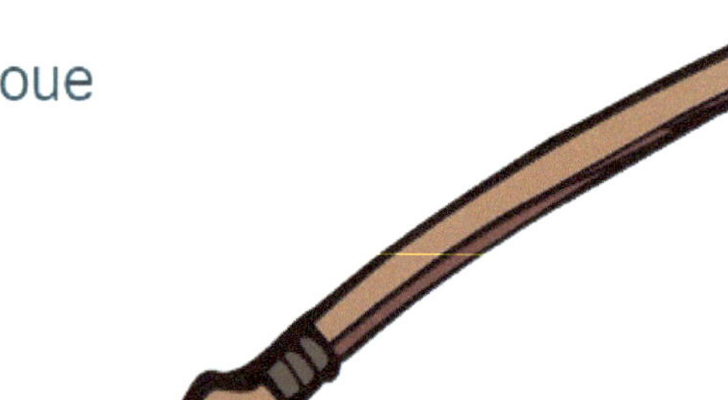

water   l'eau

l'eau

agua   dwr

He is drinking water.

---

pig   porc

porc

cerdo   mochyn

She is lying on the pig.

---

horse   cheval

cheval

caballo   ceffyl

The horse is galloping.

baby

bébé

bébé

bebé

babi

The baby is crawling.

farm

ferme

ferme

granja

fferm

The farm has lots of animals.

ring

bague

bague

anillo

ffoniwch

The bird is holding a ring.

nest

nid

nid

nido

nyth

The bird has a nest.

leg

jambe

jambe

pierna

coes

My leg is feeling better.

chair

chaises

chaises

sillas

cadair

He is sitting on the chair.

stick

bâton

bâton

palo

ffon

He is playing sticks.

ball

balle

Balle

pelota

bêl

He is bouncing the ball.

bell

cloche

cloche

campana

gloch

I hear the bell ringing!

morning · matin

Matin

mañana · bore

I wake up in the morning.

brother · frère

frère

hermano · brawd

They are brothers.

floor · sol

sol

suelo · llawr

The girl sits on the floor.

four — quatre

quatre

cuatro — pedwar

There were four of them.

---

score — but

But

puntuación — sgôr

What was the final score?

---

day — journée

journée

día — Dydd

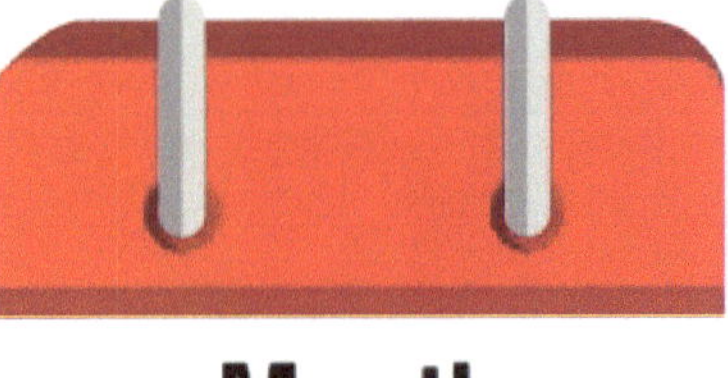

This day is the 30th.

children   les enfants

les enfants

niños   plant

Four children sang.

idea   idée

idée

idea   syniad

I have an idea!

watch   l'horloge

l'horloge

reloj   Gwylio

My watch is ticking.

milk   lait

Lait

leche   llaeth

The baby is drinking milk.

---

picture   image

image

imagen   llun

He is taking some pictures.

---

thing   chose

chose

cosa   peth

I am thinking of many things.

rope   corde

corde

cuerda   rhaff

Do you have any rope?

---

night   nuit

nuit

noche   nos

We sleep at night.

---

squirrel   écureuil

écureuil

ardilla   wiwer

The squirrel is on the tree.

farmer

fermier

fermier

agricultor

ffermwr

The farmer had a farm.

table

table

table

mesa

bwrdd

There is a toy on the table.

house

maison

maison

casa

tŷ

We live in the same house.

coat   manteau

manteau

saco   cot

She is wearing her coat.

---

bread   pain

pain

un pan   bara

She is baking some bread.

---

home   maison

maison

casa   adref

He drew a picture of his home.

bear   ours

ours

oso   arth

The bear likes to eat honey.

rabbit   lapin

lapin

conejo   cwningen

The rabbit wants to play.

conditions   conditions

conditions

condiciones   amodau

What are the weather conditions.

father   père

père

papá   tad

He is a nice father.

snow   neige

neige

nieve   eira

I have fun in the snow.

door   porte

porte

puerta   drws

He is knocking on the door.

dog   chien 

chien

perro   ci

The dog wants to eat sweets.

---

seat   siège 

siège

asiento   sedd

The girls took a seat in the sand.

---

city   ville 

ville

ciudad   ddinas

He worked in the city.

men — hommes

Hommes

hombres — dynion

The men are arguing.

---

corn — blé

blé

maíz — corn

I grow corn in the garden.

---

cat — chat

chat

gato — cath

That cat is adorable.

fête

party   fête

fête

fiesta   parti

I love to go to parties.

exemple

example   exemple

exemple

ejemplo   enghraifft

This is an example of a bird.

aliments

food   aliments

aliments

comida   bwyd

They made a lot of food.

sheep

mouton

mouton

oveja

defaid

The sheep have fluffy wool.

---

school

école

école

colegio

ysgol

They are going to school.

---

fresh

frais

Frais

fresco

ffres

All the fruit is fresh.

duck   canard

canard

pato   hwyaden

The duck is swimming.

---

wood   bois

bois

madera   pren

He plays with wooden blocks

Greek   grec

grec

griego   Groeg

Have you ever had Greek food?

money   argent

argent

dinero   arian

I save money in my piggy bank.

---

hand   main

main

mano   llaw

You should wash your hands.

---

doll   poupée

poupée

muñeca   dol

She is hugging her doll.

chicken   poulet

poulet

pollo   cyw iâr

The chicken is laying eggs.

---

office   bureau

Bureau

oficina   swyddfa

Do you need any office supplies?

---

column   colonne

colonne

columna   colofn

Did you read the newspaper column?

shoe   chaussure

chaussure

zapato   esgid

I have new shoes.

---

way   façon

façon

camino   ffordd

They find a way back home.

---

car   voiture

voiture

coche   car

My car is fast

rain   pluie

pluie

lluvia   glaw

We love the rain!

---

feet   pieds

pieds

pies   traed

His feet are swollen.

---

company   compagnie

compagnie

empresa   cwmni

What company do you work for?

fire

feu

Feu

fuego

tân

Fire is hot.

---

grass

herbe

herbe

césped

glaswellt

The goat is eating the grass.

---

seed

la graine

la graine

semilla

Hedyn

We will plant the seeds.

face   visage

visage

cara   wyneb

They were at the face painting booth.

---

church   église

église

iglesia   eglwys

Did you go to church?

---

nose   nez

nez

nariz   trwyn

My nose is running.

girl   fille

fille

niña   merch

The girl is pretty.

bed   lit

lit

cama   gwely

We all share three beds.

rose   rose

Rose

rosa   Rhosyn

Thank you for the rose.

chart   graphique

graphique

gráfico   siart

What does your medical chart say?

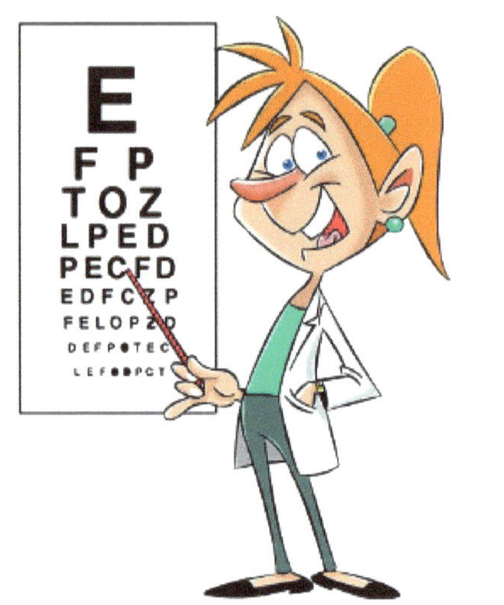

---

game   jeu

Jeu

juegos   gêm

What game is it?

---

cotton   coton

coton

algodón   cotwm

A q-tip is made of cotton.

children — les enfants

les enfants

niños — plant

The children are playing.

mother — mère

mère

madre — mam

My mother loves me.

France — france

France

francia — Ffrainc

Have you ever been to France?

birthday — anniversaire

anniversaire

cumpleaños — pen-blwydd

Today is my birthday.

---

tree — arbre

arbre

árbol — coeden

She is sitting under a tree.

---

song — chanson

chanson

canciones — cân

She is singing a song.

name	nom

Nom

nombre	enw

My name is Joe.

---

egg	oeuf

Oeuf

huevo	wy

The bunny has many eggs.

---

oxygen	oxygène

oxygène

oxígeno	ocsigen

O_2

What is the symbol for oxygen?

letter — alphabet

alphabet

alfabeto — llythyr

Learn English letters is fun.

top — haut

Haut

tapas — brig

We like to play with tops.

boy — garçon

garçon

chico — bachgen

The boy is eating dinner.

eye   œil

œil

ojo   llygad

He is closing his eyes.

---

time   temps

temps

hora   amser

He is telling the time.

---

kitty   minou

minou

gatito   Kitty

I like my kitty.

garden

jardin

jardin

jardín

gardd

They are going to the garden.

sun

soleil

Soleil

dom

haul

The sun is very bright.

apple

pomme

Pomme

manzana

afal

Apples are a popular fruit.

wind

vent

vent

viento

gwynt

The wind blows the leaves.

boat

bateau

bateau

barco

cwch

The boat is sailing.

page

page

page

página

tudalen

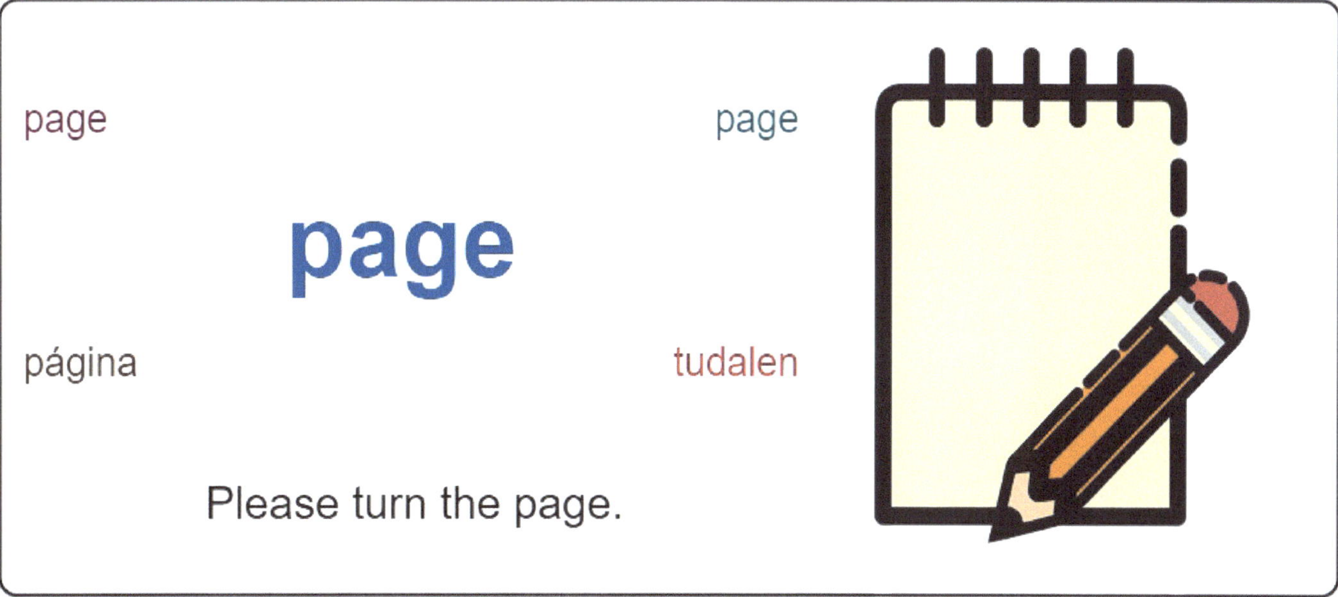

Please turn the page.

cake   gâteau

gâteau

pastel   cacen

The cake is white and pink.

---

paper   papier

papier

papel   papur

I like to color on paper.

---

goodbye   au revoir

Au revoir

adiós   Hwyl fawr

The bear is saying goodbye.

sister   sœur

sœur

hermana   chwaer

She is my sister.

---

box   boîte

boîte

caja   blwch

The box is full of clothes.

---

head   tête

tête

cabeza   pen

She has a hat on her head.

window   fenêtre

fenêtre

ventana   ffenestr

The window is open.

fish   poisson

poisson

pez   pysgod

There are two fish.

cow   vache

vache

vaca   buwch

The cow is standing up.

gun — pistolet

pistolet

pistola — gwn

We played with a water gun.

hill — colline

colline

colina — bryn

The house is on the hill.

bird — oiseau

oiseau

pájaro — aderyn

The bird is dancing happily.

ground   sol

sol

suelo   ddaear

It plays a trick on the ground.

robin   robin

Robin

robin   robin goch

The robin is helping Santa.

street   rue

rue

calle   stryd

They walk across the street.

place

endroit

endroit

sitio

lle

This is my favorite place.

flower

fleur

fleur

flor

blodyn

She is holding a flower.

toy

jouet

jouet

juguete

tegan

He has a whole box of toys.